THE LORD IS A MAN OF WAR

LADEJOLA ABIODUN

THE LORD IS A MAN OF WAR

Ladejola Abiodun

Copyright © 2020 Ladejola Abiodun

All rights reserved. No part of this publication may be reproduced, stored in a retrieval system or transmitted in any form or by any means, electronic, mechanical, photocopying, recording or otherwise, without prior permission of the author.

THANK YOU FOR YOUR SUPPORT!

Thank you for choosing this book and investing in your spiritual growth. As my gift to you, I'm offering 4 additional ebooks packed with powerful prayers and declarations to strengthen your faith. Don't miss out—download them now and experience even more blessings!

Scan QR Code to download or visit:

HTTPS://LADEJOLAABIODUN.ORG/GIFT

CONTENTS

Also from Ladejola Abiodun   v
Introduction   ix

1. God Will Stand By The Just   1
2. Own Up And Apologize   3
3. O God, Arise In Your True Power   5
4. Who Dares To Challenge God?   9
5. Enemies Of Your Progress   13
6. Deliverance From Being Tied To A Spot   17
7. Dangerous Environmental Powers   23
8. Requirements For Victory   39
9. Required Sacrifice For Victory   41

Also from Ladejola Abiodun   43

ALSO FROM LADEJOLA ABIODUN

Here are some of the other books written by Ladejola Abiodun:

The God of Possibility

You Cannot Give Up Now

No More Delay

This book is dedicated to God Almighty, the giver of all knowledge and our Saviour, the Lord Jesus Christ.

INTRODUCTION

The Lord is a man of war, there is no battle that scares God.

Your problems and the enemies that have gathered against you do not scare Him. Rather battles make God excited.

The bible says in Exodus 15:3 *"The Lord is a man of war, the Lord is his name"*. *He is not afraid of any enemy. Deuteronomy 32:4 also says "He is the Rock, his work is perfect; for all his ways are just: a God of truth and without iniquity, just and right is He"*.

This book shows you how to prepare yourself in order to cause God to arise, fight and win the battles of life for you!

God bless you.

Ladejola Abiodun

1

GOD WILL STAND BY THE JUST

Many people come into the presence of God to tell lies forgetting that God, who is omnipresent, saw them perpetrating ugly actS. He knows you and you must be upright if you want Him to fight for you. He is not a God of perversion.

Whoever is just, God will stand by him. No matter whom you are, if you are right and just, he will stand and fight for you. It does not matter the number of people that had come against you. It does not matter your status or stature. You may not be a rich man, you may be an orphan, you may be lowly placed, young or even unpopular but you are just and truthful, God will stand by you.

Imagine, Mordecai and Haman. Who was Mordecai? He was a gateman while Hamman was a cabinet minister. Haman had the heart of the king; in short, he was the next to be king. When both of them had rift, whom do you think God pitched his tent with, of course the gateman named

Mordecai because he is a just God. There are people who come to church with very wicked heart. The crookedness in their heart is unimaginable, how can God fight for such people when they are full of wickedness.

You have to search your heart. If you are bent on your wicked ways, don't expect God to contend with them that contend with you, but if you want God to fight for you and always be on your side, kindly humble yourself and reconcile with God. Many have become superficial; some of you can sense that the oil of God had left you. Every thing you are doing is just to fulfill all righteousness. Where did you miss God, go back there because God is ready. Things are going to be overturned.

There is going to be a quick move, the power of God is ready. Tell me who can stand in his way.

There are womanizers in our fold; some ladies go to church from the house of someone who is not their husband. There are husband's snatchers in the church. They are using prayer points to snatch someone else's husband. There are people who collect or borrow things from others, to pay or give those things back becomes an issue. When they want to borrow money they will beg with sweet tongue but paying back is totally a different kettle of fish. When the person asks for his money, he will say "is it because of such and such amount that you want to kill somebody".

That is not how to live. You must be just and upright. You must be truthful, if you want the Lord on your side.

2

OWN UP AND APOLOGIZE

If you want God to be interested in your matter, then stop pilling up lies by covering one lie with another, and never owning up.

Why is it difficult for Christians to own up? When they make a mistake instead of owning up and apologizing, they will start backbiting and backstabbing from one person to another. At end of the day, he is the culprit. Come to think of it, if you can tell lies in the presence of your Pastor, who would you tell the truth? God can scarcely help you under this condition, except you confess and own up.

Every power behind your problems will bow every enemy that is holding your life to ransom must bow. All the evil trends, evil occurrences, within this period, those stretched battles, prolonged warfare, difficult issues of life, those stubborn problems shall receive permanent termination. Some of us have some medical issues, typical problems, sicknesses and diseases. All the things that are plaguing your life, God will plague them and give you rest.

The powers that are making it difficult for you to settle down, not to make reasonable progress in life, there shall be mass burial for all of them in the mighty name of Jesus.

It is time for everyone to know who God is. Elijah told them there was no need to debate on this issue further, he challenged them go to mount Camel to determine who is who, and when they got there, the true God surfaced. Fire will fall down. Your enemies who make things difficult for you must bow. If they don't repent, their obituary would be announced.

3

O GOD, ARISE IN YOUR TRUE POWER

We live in a world where people boast of what they have acquired. Many have acquired evil powers and they are looking for others whom they will afflict with such vicious powers. That is more reason why some people go about looking for trouble, challenging whoever crosses their path.

In a recent lecture on International Relations, the issues in relations between USA and USSR were extensively discussed. They are world's super powers. The intractable cold war has ushered in a season of strategic militaiy initiatives resulting in massive development of weapons of mass destruction by both super powers. When USA, for instance, goes to smaller nations and causes them to wage war against another nation, promising them sophisticated weapons, USSR too, will stir up the other nation and promise to supply them with modem weapons of warfare, but the two super powers would never fight against each other. They want to test their weapons of modem warfare in those conflicts they stirred up.

In the same vein, those who have acquired evil powers often stir up disharmony and challenge anybody standing in their way to enable them test their latest charms on the unsuspecting fellow. They boast about it. "I will make sure you eat from the dust bin". Have you not heard people boast in that manner? The people that make this type of threat have evil backing. The bible says they trusted in their chariot and horses. They trusted in their juju and talisman "I will make sure you suffer in this office, I will ensure that you are not promoted in this office" Is he God? Does he know what will happen the next day? The Psalmist said why do the nations rage and the people imagine a vain thing?

One brother was doing well, he offended his uncle. The uncle threatened that he would deal with the brother and of course he dealt with him devastatingly to the extent that he ran out of this country. Before his escape he lost his business, he was begging to eat, as if that was not enough he lost one eye before he escaped. Unfortunately, you don't have to run for the enemy. Otherwise he will become stubborn in the pursuit. If you go to Europe, you see many people who ran away from home. Somebody chased them away. Somebody threatened them with evil powers. On their own part, they imagined that once they escape abroad, their problem would end. They have since discovered otherwise, because the demons are no respecter of boundaries or distance, in other words they check into the flight with you.

4

WHO DARES TO CHALLENGE GOD?

There are powers that boast and brag but no one can boast or brag against the Lord God and get away with it. Check their list from the time of old. People like Pharoah who said he did not know and does not want to know Him ended up in a body of waters not even on burial ground or cemetery. Sennacharib was disgraced and humiliated and died a miserable death. Nebuchadnezzar became an animal and ran into the bush for seven years. By the time he came back, his vocabulary changed. He can even pass as the greatest king, that worshiped God the most.

There was a presidential candidate in Brazil who boasted that if he could get up to 500,000 votes from his party not even God can stop him from being the president of Brazil. Just look of this type of statement. Do you know what happened, few days after the election where he secured well over 500,000 votes, before he could be sworn in as the president he died. When the Titanic was built, one of the reporters interviewed the engineers who boasted about the superiority of the titanic. He said that even God cannot sink that ship. What happened, the titanic hit an iceberg and got capsized with thousands of souls on her maiden voyage.

There was a man called John Lennon, he said in an interview with one American magazine that he was more popular than Jesus, six days after he died. A group of boys and girls wanted to have fun by cruising around the city after being drunk. The mother of one of the boys was a Christian; she sensed that these young people were already drunk. He called his son and gave him bible in other to just mellow the guys down. The boys told his mother that God has no place in that car. Halfway into the journey, they had accident and all died. It was discovered that in the booth of the car where they kept the bible, that even the crate of egg inside there was not affected. In short God protected the egg and the bible. No one has ever boasted against the Lord and got away with it.

A musician sang in February 1980, that "I am going all the way down to the high way of hell. Few days after, he was found dead and quickly descended to hell. There was one lady that once said that bible is the worst book she had ever read. She prophesized that soonest, bible would disappear. She was a journalist. She physically burnt many bibles few days after, she was found dead inside her vehicle.

No one has ever challenged the Lord God and survived. God does not take such insult from anybody. The bible says that Herod arrogated the power due to God to himself and sat on his throne and took the position of God. He made the people to begin to hail him. They said his voice was like that of God. God knew that Herod had gone too far and sent one angel that gave Herod a knock and he died. That is how God will knockout your stubborn pursuers. What happened to Herod? He did not die immediately. It was recorded that maggot started coming out from that spot he got that knock. So he shamefully died little by little. All those who hate you, who want you to go down, who had vowed that you will pick your food from the dust bin, those who are going from one altar to another to tie you down, would receive the knock of an angel individually and collectively in the mighty name of Jesus.

Who is a witch, herbalists, an enchanter, a palm reader, necromancer, magician, idol worshiper, rainmakers? They cannot stand in the presence of the almighty God. I want to challenge you to be serious with God. Repair your altars with God because fire cannot fall if your altars are already polluted. Make sure there is no dark spot because the devil an accuser of the brethren.

5

ENEMIES OF YOUR PROGRESS

If you don't believe there are enemies, it is dangerous for you.

There are enemies that have covenanted their souls to the devil and have vowed that progress would be veiy difficult for you, that you cannot make it. Did you offend them? Even if you offend them. The bible says there is no way you will live in this world without offense. You will offend somebody and vice versa. Does it mean that the person should die because he offended you? Is there no room for forgiveness? Is there no room for mercy and second chance? Why do you want to destroy somebody, just because he offended you? Some people are after your life because they say your parents offended them and they refuse to forgive your parents and now they are carrying this battle over to you.

To some people it is just envy that is driving them. When you ask him what this person did to him, he will say nothing so the problem is envy and bitterness because God is blessing you. There are people who cannot just see you being blessed; they cannot understand why it should be you. They ask why you are still alive. Why haven't you packed to the village? Why are you not a beggar yet? Why must you be the one that is being promoted?

Why must you be the one that is being lifted up? Why did Cain kill Abel? Cain could not handle the blessing of Abel. There are people like that. How can you be wearing fine clothes? They expect you to cook Amala and come to beg them for Ewedu that is when they accept you. If you want to go somewhere and ask them for transport money, they will be happy for your condition. Look at you, how can you buy car? God blessed that brother; he executed a contract and was able to buy a new car.

He parked the car in front of his house. When his enemies saw the car, they concluded it could not be his. Where would he get such money, may be it is his friends car by the evening time they will drive off. But the car stayed put! The next day the car was still there. They went to the police and reported that the young man was a thief, but the report came to naught. Who are these people that have written you off? Have concluded that you cannot amount to anything? Has the enemy said you cannot be more than this? Is the enemy already sitting on you? They are rejoicing and saying "we have captured him". Who are these powers, who are these wicked people? Who are these witches and wizards? Let fire fall on them and destroy them in the name of Jesus. The psalmist said, "They hate me without a cause" he did not do any thing to them. But they hated him without a cause.

They will smile at you physically, but bite you in the back. They will dress up in your shoes and clothes and still carry false news about you. Somebody was sitting by the side of her friend in the church and the man of God was preaching suddenly the spirit of the Lord said something to the man of God and he walked down to one of the sisters and asked her "Sister where is your husband? "He had left home" He asked her, "Since when?" the madam answered "Far back". Suddenly the man of God turned to her friend who was sitting by her side "Did you hear what your friend said, what is your comment?" She answered, "Man of God, it is true", "Did you have anything to do with the man's departure?" asked the man of God. The woman denied "man of God nothing oh!". The man of God asked her to bring her cell phone, she surrendered the handset and he scrolled down to the text message sent by the other ladies "missing" husband. The text message read: "When you will be coming in the evening, buy banana and groundnut and meet me at room X of hotel Y. That is her friend, they eat together, attend the same church. Who is this stranger that seeks to destroy you in the back but laugh with you physically? Let fire answer them in the name of Jesus.

DELIVERANCE FROM BEING TIED TO A SPOT

Why is that some people, are not doing well? In a family, the father, the children, no one is doing well, every body is stagnant. Are you tied somewhere? There are people who are tied such that they cannot go beyond certain limit. A full grown man, no matter his strength, his exposure, despite his academic prowess, irrespective of his ability and capability, if he is tied to a spot, there is nothing he can do anymore. In the case of the colt that was tied in Mark 11:2, Jesus sent his disciples to go and loose him. If you are tied by any means with any unseen evil rope, heaven will lose you today in the mighty name of Jesus.

Jesus told them to "loose him in case there was challenge, tell them the master needs it". True to this anticipation, people accosted them and demanded to know why they should loose the colt. The truth of the matter was that they were somewhere monitoring what shall become of the colt, waiting to see who may attempt to lose it. Do you know they may be monitoring you to the effect that anywhere you want to go; they will be there even before you. Evil monitors, evil escorts, wicked powers. If you are being followed about, you are being monitored, receive your deliverance now by fire by thunder in the mighty name of Jesus Christ.

A brother saw the type of wickedness in the village and relocated to town. He was blessed and so he bought a car, before then any time he wants to go to the village, he would dress shabbily to give the impression of bad condition. But as time progressed, God continued to bless him, so he bought a car. When he wanted to travel to village, he parked his car in the village next to his own and trekked to his own village. He slept over and in the morning, his uncle came to greet him and congratulated him on the lofty achievement of purchasing a car. The brother asked him "Congratulation for what? He replied "For the new car you bought" the brother said "Which car"? The uncle laughed. He told him that they saw him and where he parked the car; the man was flabbergasted in bewilderment. The uncle told the man to peep through the hole in the stick he was walking with and behold he saw his car securely parked in the village next to theirs. Who is monitoring your life, they shall expire in the name of Jesus. There was a particular church. You know there are different types of churches. There is psychedelic church where they call God "Gad" before the pastor comes to preach he will tell you the Greek or Hebrew meaning of the topic of the day.

DELIVERANCE FROM BEING TIED TO A SPOT

They call God the father "Fado" until one day, they invited a preacher. The man collected the microphone and began to bind all the witches and wizard within the vicinity. The host pastor became upset because according to him "we don't believe in all those things".

The guest pastor called one prayer point, the ladies who were on the front row whose fingernails were very long and colourful began to summersault. It was the second prayer point that caused trouble. The mother of the pastor started confessing. The pastor who was upset and visibly angered by the prayer point against witches and wizards opened his eyes and saw what was happening. His own mother started confessing that she was the one behind the problem of that pastor. To cut the long story short the pastor forgot about brokeness, loosed the belt of his trouser and was changing the Mother within the church. This experience changed the Pastor's theology. From that day, he became an ardent prayer warrior.

Many people have confused their bible reading and turned it upside down. They said that Jesus enjoined us to pray for our enemies. Did he tell you the kind of prayer you will pray? Jesus is the only person, who is qualified to say to his enemies "they know not what they are doing" They were helping him to fulfill his dream and prophecy. In our own situation today, are we going to be hung on the cross? Does the present enemy of our soul help in any way to accomplish any good thing?

They are making mockery of your salvation. They want

the life of holiness you are living to become questionable. They are asking where your God is. They want to make your salvation to lose value. They are saying all these times you have been carrying bible around, where has it led you to? God will settle these matters very soon.

If you want to live, prepare to fight, the demons here are not like the demons in Europe and America, please note this. But the local demons have become incorrigibly wicked.

A lady was admitted for child delivery, all effort for the baby to come forth failed. The Oyibo man who was the resident doctor at the hospital had spent reasonable time in Nigeria, he has been used to the way and manner such things happen in this country. When all efforts failed, he asked to see the person that came with the lady, they called the mother in-law but she refused to follow them, they came back and told the doctor that the woman refused to come and see him. The doctor sensed danger and decided to go to where the woman was sitting. He asked her to get up but the woman refused. It was obvious to the doctor that something was wrong; so he called the security and some boys and asked them to lift the woman up. People of God this was a true life story, not dream or script. When they forcefully lifted the woman up, it was found that she was sitting on a particular cloth which the Yoruba people call "Osuka", a piece of cloth mainly used in carrying heavy loads on the head. Immediately they lifted her up, the baby came out forcefully.

Any power that is holding your destiny to ransom, any power that is chanting incantation against your well being, any powers that is standing naked on any evil altar to bring you down, powers that have visited evil shrines to tie your glory, they shall expire in the name of Jesus.

DANGEROUS ENVIRONMENTAL POWERS

When we looked at the evil altar, we noted that the majority of the problems people face in our environment is the problem from the evil altar. We defined and explored the meaning of evil altar. Let us now consider the seven most dangerous powers in our environment and what we shall do to effectively deal with them.

Seven Most Dangerous Powers in Our Environment

1. Witchcraft

Every story we have shared about witchcraft is not a figment of my imagination, it is a real life story that, has happened to somebody. Although most people find it difficult to understand, if they listen to what other people are going through, they will begin to appreciate the subject matter. Witchcraft is being practiced everywhere, here in Africa and elsewhere in the world. There is witchcraft in Diaspora, but the wickedness that is demonstrated by witchcraft in our environment has already proved that the type of witches and wizards we have here are unrepentant and incorrigibly despicable.

When you come to our environment, you will see hardened and brutal witchcraft practitioners. In the United States, they will not block you from having a baby but in this our locality, they will bury stone inside the womb that is supposed to incubate a child. They exchange human brain with that of goat. In Western countries, people apply witchcraft in space shuttling, developing breath taking technologies, all kinds of aircraft, missiles, war heads. African witches and wizards would not venture into such inventions; rather they would use human beings as their own mode of transportation. They would ride a human being to the venue of their meeting. They prey on human beings, eat flesh like bread and drink blood like water, that informed the saying of the psalmist (in Psalm 27:2) that when his enemies came to eat his flesh, they will stumble and fall. One thing is that we will not be meat in the mouth of any witch. No witch or wizard shall drink our blood, in the name of Jesus.

We have so much to talk about in witchery and wizardry. The kind of wickedness the witches and wizards have done to many destinies is unimaginable.

Somebody travelled abroad, and was doing well there. He came from a polygamous family and decided to help one of his nephews being kind hearted. The mother of that nephew called her son and told him that he would travel to be with his brother overseas, that his brother would come and welcome him at the airport. "See this thing, take it and hide it around your waist, as soon as he comes to embrace you there, every thing he has, every virtue, will be transferred to you". This evil plan came to lime light because while he was still waiting to board the aircraft, for one reason or the other, the flight was delayed that was how their evil plan boomeranged and backfired. Who ever is planning your down fall, after eating your food, and drinking your water, it will back fire seven fold in Jesus name.

2. Marine witchcraft

When you hear marine, then the subject has to do with water. The water kingdom is a terrible place. It is the headquarters of wickedness, people of God. There is another life inside the water. Things go on there just like it goes on here. There is something that is called the kingdom of waters, look at Exodus 20:4 "Thou shall have no other gods before me. Thou shall not make unto thee any graven image or any likeness of anything that is in heaven above or that is in the earth beneath or that is in the water under the earth. There are people who tap power from the water.

Pharaoh got his powers from the water that was why the first plague was an attack against the waters, and against all other gods in Egypt. Every morning, Pharaoh would go to river Nile to bathe. Come to think of it, why would a whole king go to the river to bathe when he had all kinds of bathing equipment in the comfort of his house? Even the daughter of Pharaoh went to the same river on daily basis to shower ostensibly. They go there to renew covenant and acquire more powers. That was why God first of all attacked their waters when He decided to afflict Egypt. Eventually Pharaoh perished inside water just the same way the sword of Goliath was used to behead him. Those who are hunting for your life, the grave they dug for you, shall be used for their burial in the mighty name of Jesus.

What about python spirit? When you come to the place of deliverance and see the person with python spirit displaying by thrusting out his tongue as done by python. The mermaid would be swimming on the floor as if she is inside the water, when you call fire prayer she can swim from one end to the other, on a hard concrete, that is water spirit. When you hear Dragon, it is also water spirit. When you hear Leviathan that is another wicked spirit. The bible called it boasting serpent, it says "who can kill me who can capture me", they boast in their powers.

Water spirit is a proud spirit. When you hear of divination, the spirit of divination is water spirit. When you read Act 16: 6 you read about that little girl that was following Paul around, she was prophesying "these are the servants of the most high God, who have come to show us the way of salvation". She was operating under the spirit of divination They have the ability to see. These people when you enter their houses, they will say young man, your father married three wives, your mother is the second one. Your father died three years ago, and he could not complete the project he was building in the village. They will give accurate data about you and your family. It is the spirit of divination. They can see anything. Many people would assume that if he knows this much about them, he is then in the best position to help him out. They cannot help you even though he gives you this information. When they allege that somebody is a witch, don't dispute it because they are witches themselves.

You may not know that there is a place called the water kingdom, but the politicians know, they equally know that when you are looking for power and you lave not visited them forget it. Those who are looking for blood money knows. Many aesthetic and wonderful designs we see today came from the water kingdom.

Many years ago, a lady was delivered from the hold of marine spirit, she confessed that by the function of this deliverance, she has been stranded, she said anytime she want to go out, all she need to do was to just dress and walk up to the street, a car will come and take her to wherever she want to go. Many who are complaining about things moving in their body, sickness that comes and goes, seasonal sicknesses, always swimming in the dream, for sure that is attack from water spirit. Having sex in the dream is caused by water spirit. They mastermind devastating tornadoes; hurricanes and tsunamis. They afflict their victims with insanity; sometimes they threatened the members who want to be delivered with outright madness and death.

. . .

3. Curses

This is another terrible power that has to do with generational curses, family curses, individual curses, curses of misfortunes different kinds of curses. Inability to do well in life, spirit of failure, bad luck, all kinds of trouble, are resultant effects curses.

Gehazi, was afflicted with the curse leprosy instead of receiving double portion blessing from Elisha. Joseph told Rueben, "you will not excel", and so it was a curse of not excelling in life, there could be the curse of barenness, failure and poverty.

A curse could be upon a person and he would be prone to accident, anywhere he goes he must have accident, even if he is inside the house. Whatever curse is plaguing your life, let it be broken now, in the mighty name of Jesus.

Prayer points:

1. The rage of marine witchcraft assigned against me die, in Jesus name.

2. Every marine witchcraft embargo in my success, break to pieces in Jesus name.

3. Every fountain of sorrow in my life, dry up in Jesus name.

4. Any man or woman using marine witchcraft power to subdue my destiny expire by fire.

5. Altar, shrine, grooves attacking my prosperity catch fire.

6. Every Object, image representing me at the marine altar catch fire in Jesus name.

7. My season of unending laughter manifest in Jesus name.

4. Foundational bondage

You cannot separate a person from his place of birth, his father, his mother, and the environments. You cannot separate a person from these variables and they are the factors that determine how far we can go and the speed of our progress in life. Can a man whose placenta is buried under a tree in the village do well?

There was this story of a man who had committed many atrocities to make stupendous wealth. He had many children among who were twenty girls that had gotten married. The man built a house behind his main house made up of single room apartment fondly called "face me, I face you house". His daughters who left their various husbands homes returned to their father's compound and settled in those rooms. In the evenings, all manner of men will be coming around the house. The one with Mercedes Benz V. Boot will pick, the one with Beetle will pick and drop. The place had become a hotel or better still a brothel.

We cannot separate a person from his place of birth. The bible says, if the foundation be destroyed what could the righteous do. The righteous can repair the foundation through repentance, deliverance and prayers. When you discover that you are not doing well in life, under the circumstances in which you find yourself, you have examined the left, right and center, it is not because you are not working hard, not because opportunities are not coming your way, many people are surrounded with great opportunities but they are not able to use it. It is because of foundational bondage.

Prayer points:

1. Every conscious or unconscious covenant I have inherited or acquired be broken in Jesus name.

2. I pull down every stronghold of delay working against me.

3. Anti progress power, anti success power pursing my destiny, die.

4. Satanic limit or satanic barrier programmed in my way of success catch fire.

5. Jehovah the man of war, fight for me, trouble my trouble.

6. Where is the Lord God of Elijah, disgrace the evil altar of my father's house.

7. Arrow of nightmare fired against me from my place of birth catch fire.

8. Every bitter water flowing into my life dry up by fire in Jesus name.

5. Evil Altars

Evil altar is as terrible as anyone can imagine. The problem of evil altar in our environment is deeper than anyone can fathom. Look at Judges 6:25 "and it came to pass that same night that the Lord said unto him take thy fathers young bullock even the second bullock of seven years old and throw down the altars of Baal that your father has and cut down the idol pole that is by it and built the altar of the Lord thy God on top of this rock in the ordered place and take the second bullock and offer a burnt sacrifice with the wood of the idol pole which you shall cut down".

This was the story of Gideon, a young man that wanted to succeed in life. He possibly might have graduated with B.Sc, MBA or their equivalent. He may have had his plans well laid out but each time he makes an attempt to move forward, something drags him back. Any time he maps out a plan, it scatters, Gideon started asking questions, started praying, and God spoke to him. Do you know why your life was like this, it is the altar of your father's house. If you must make progress, you must pull it down and build another one.

The bible recorded that Gideon went in the night and dismantled the altar. When they woke up in the morning, behold, the altar of Baal, was already leveled to the ground. The worshipers of Baal came to the father of Gideon and told him that his son had done abomination and so must die. The father of Gideon was a wise man; he asked them whether they want to fight for the gods. If the idol is strong, let it fight for himself. It was after that exercise that Gideon became a force to reckon with in the bible and eventually fulfilled his destiny. In our environment, there are different types of altars, the church altar, it is believed that that is where the concentration of power is, there is community altar, personal altar and family altar. Markets in our environment have altar. Before a market is set up, an ancestral altar is raised somewhere. Some of these altars are still speaking death to some people's life. Many of the houses where most of us live were built on altars. We need to cry unto the Lord, we need to pull down stronghold as Gideon did. We need to render the demons behind these altars powerless so that our life shall be progressive.

There are different kinds of altar in our environment. A man of God went inside the bush to pray. He was a kind of man of God who understands these deliverance messages. As he was praying something told him to look up, he saw a tree full of nails and something told him to pull off the nails. As he pulled off the nails, behold there was a piece of paper, with somebody's name written on it that was nailed to the tree. Who knows whether the person or persons whose names appeared on those papers had gone for deliverance at one place or the other, and God had used this man of God to release them.

Altars in our environment

Cross road altar: That is where two roads meet, what they do is to summon power from the North South East and West. Also when you get to the cross roads you see sacrifices, you see fresh chicken, coconut, rice, even biscuits and minerals, somebody has offered to the evil spirit. People do all kinds of thing like that at a cross road.

Cemetery Altar: In our environment cemetery is supposed to be the resting place of the dead, but not now, the cemetery attendant would tell you the number and status of their clients. These visitors seek audience with the spirits, to collect power from the environment and speak with the death. They would not allow the death to rest, some even sleep there. Those who are looking for money would find the grave of a rich man, they will go and sleep there and make all kind of incantation.

Somebody was confessing how intolerant the power from the cemetery could be. If they ask you to do something and you fail to carry it out exactly, the person would be slain immediately. There are many occultists, satanic agents, diabolics, satanic prophets, Satanists. Those who are looking for power, protection and of course those who want to hurt others also go there. It is possible that you do not know that what belong to you has been taken to the grave.

Every grave yard altars speaking destruction against your life catch fire in the name of Jesus.

6. The Evil Tree

The bible tells us that there is tree of death and tree of life. Humanity ran into trouble because they ate the wrong fruit and God quickly chased them away from the garden before they could lay their hand on the very tree of life so they will not die again. Also Proverb 3:18 talks about the tree of life. Trees are so important in our human life and

Endeavour. We have one thing or the other that we do with trees.

Economic purposes of Trees: We use tree to build houses and make furniture, but more than this, people have discovered that tree have certain powers. In the villages there are trees you mention their names with awe and sanctity. There are trees that once you mention its name people believe it is a dangerous tree. There are trees that refuse to fall when the people want to cut it down, there are others that bleed with blood while being cut. While cutting some trees, the cut out part keep replacing itself. Dangerous trees that is. There are trees that any body who attempts to cut them down shall die. In one outstanding case, the Dolma engine used in attempting to cut the tree got knocked.

There are families, the moment a child is born, especially a male child, a tree is planted. The implication is that the life of the child is going to be controlled by that tree, if the tree is experiencing dryness, the child will be experiencing dryness. If there is a whirlwind that blows the tree then the life of that man would be swinging like a pendulum. When they mention Iroko tree, banana tree, pawpaw tree, it is a common belief that these are trees where witches and wizards hold meetings. They have used these types of trees to waste many lives and destinies. If there is any tree anywhere responsible for your condition now, the tree will catch fire and burn to ashes in the mighty name of our Lord Jesus Christ.

7. The Image Altar

That is where they mould something in the form of an image and put it on the altar. They deposit certificate, pieces of clothes, pictures, sands from under your feet, they form a statute which personifies someone and whatever they do to that statute will affect the person being represented by it.

A woman who was mysteriously delivered testified that she got pregnant, then five months into that pregnancy, she discovered that one of her clothes was missing; she prayed and asked people to pray for her. By the ninth month, the baby refused to come. She cried and prayed the more, different people kept praying. On the 11th month, she was rushed to the hospital and the baby started coming. Push! The baby brought out the head but behold the cloth of the woman that was missing about six months ago was used to wrap that baby.

That was what covered the baby. Who knows what could have happened if that woman has not been a prayer warrior. It could have been one of those ectopic or toxeamic pregnancies, eclampsia and preeclampsia disorders, which could culminated to maternal and child mortality. A lot of people are suffering like that today. God will visit those altars once again and fight for you.

There is crystal ball altar, rock altar, family altar and astral altar. Some people embark on astral travel by leaving their bodies for a meeting or to attack someone else; at the end they come back and enter their bodies again. It has happened before. This, woman was pregnant but her husband had always used this pregnancy to donate at meetings or for other evil purposes. Somebody advised her that anytime she notices the disappearance of her pregnancy again, she should come to the church for prayers. So she came for prayers. When the person that carried the pregnancy returned to deposit it back into her, she was not around, she had gone to church and that was what got the trouble bursted.

Whoever has gone on an evil meeting against your destiny shall not return in Jesus name.

Child of God, this is a time to be on fire for the Lord, the world is becoming more terrible. You don't have to be bad before they attack you. A sister showed me the text that was sent to her. In the text message, they told the sister that they have submitted her name to a particular temple, that she would die on a certain date, but she did not die eventually, because she belonged to a fire place, she replied the text message and confirmed to them that they are the ones to die. All kinds of strange thing are happening now, if you see this text you will be afraid if there is no fire in you. You need to know the God that you serve. A brother was going somewhere and along the road one prophet stood before him and shouted to him "Hey, before seven days, you will die" the brother told him "is that so" and fired back at the prophet "I have also been informed that you are the one to die within seven days".

If some of us receive that type of prophecy we shall begin

to shake and start running helter-skelter. They are all over the places; they collect your money and things like that. It is becoming a dangerous trend. People wake up in the morning to find sacrifices at the entrances of their houses.

Prayer points

1. Satanic dedication speaking failure into my life, die.

2. Environmental witchcraft altar delegated to supervise oppression against me, die.

3. Any situation of my life that does not glorify God expire.

4. Blood of Jesus gather all my wealth together from all the four corners of the earth.

5. Every dark power contending with my destiny, die.

6. I shall not die but live and declare the glory in Jesus name.

7. Any power assigned to frustrate me be frustrated.

REQUIREMENTS FOR VICTORY

You need to step up and be on fire for the Lord.

This is not a time to compromise at all. Get born again, be a true child of God, be a growing Christian, love to read the word of God, live a holy life, serve God. Don't just be nominal member in the church, do something for God, be committed. This is my honest advice.

You need to be full of God now.

You need the presence of God wherever you go. You should not be ashamed to be called a child of God.

Let the world know you as a child of God, carry your bible always with you.

Be very prayerful, live a holy life.

Be a true worshiper; worship him in truth and in spirit.

Wake up in the middle of the night, not praying but

singing praises to the Lord your God. It will strengthen your altar. Everyone of us has an altar, although most of these altars are so powerless and useless but if you are the kind of Christian that prays all the time, your altar will be powerful.

Worship God and sing praises to him always.

The children of the devil are not ashamed when dancing to their wicked gods. When you see a typical herbalist, those wicked ones, they will be dancing before their evil altar, praising, singing and pouring accolades to these powerless gods, they would be dancing and rolling on the floor.

We that are serving the most high God should be more pious and devoted, more proud and cheerful in terms of dancing and appreciating our Almighty God.

REQUIRED SACRIFICE FOR VICTORY

If you want your altar to be potent and powerful you must offer sacrifice. Your altar is as powerful as your sacrifice. Sacrifice can get you anything. Where prayers cannot break into, sacrifice can break through. A man is as great before God as his sacrifice. May the Lord open your eyes in the mighty name of our Lord Jesus Christ. The Lord is a Man of War

PRAYER POINTS

1. Satanic lion and dog assigned to scare me from my next level of glory, die.

2. Evil cloud over my destiny be dispersed in Jesus name.

3. Power holding evil vigil against me die.

4. The rage of the waters to paralyse me this year, die.

5. Principalities blocking my heaven die.

6. Witchcraft pursing my David die.

7. Cob web designed to keep me stagnant, catch fire.

8. Evil tailor and satanic fashion designer preparing to cloth me with shame, die.

9. You spirit of toiling, struggling without result, die.

10. The cage and the prison of the enemy release me by fire.

11. O earth, earth, earth, open and swallow all my sorrows, failures and tragedy.

12. My glory, like the rising of the sun, shine in Jesus name.

13. Every satanic government set up to afflict me be overthrown in Jesus name.

14. The Lord you a man of war, fight my battle for me today.

15. Arrow of shame fired against me back to sender.

16. Evil line drawn against me that says this is how far I will go catch fire.

17. Stubborn root of infirmity dry up in Jesus name.

18. Every mouth that has mocked me shall turn around to celebrate me.

19. Evil hands stealing from me wither in Jesus.

ALSO FROM LADEJOLA ABIODUN

Here are some of the other books written by Ladejola Abiodun:

The God of Possibility

You Cannot Give Up Now

No More Delay

THANK YOU FOR YOUR SUPPORT!

Thank you for choosing this book and investing in your spiritual growth. As my gift to you, I'm offering 4 additional ebooks packed with powerful prayers and declarations to strengthen your faith. Don't miss out—download them now and experience even more blessings!

Scan QR Code to download or visit:

HTTPS://LADEJOLAABIODUN.ORG/GIFT